M000074574

Dream
journal

Bill Johnson
Beni Johnson, Danny Silk,
Banning Liebscher, Kevin Dedmon

Cover Image by Linda Lee

DESTINY IMAGE® PUBLISHERS, INC.
P.O. Box 310, Shippensburg, PA 17257-0310
"Promoting Inspired Lives."

This book and all other Destiny Image and Destiny Image Fiction books are available at Christian bookstores and distributors worldwide.
Or reach us on the Internet: www.destinyimage.com

ISBN 13: HC 978-0-7684-0608-5

For Worldwide Distribution, Printed in the U.S.A.
1 2 3 4 5 6 7 8 9 10 11 /17 16 15 14

Dream Journal Introduction

And it shall come to pass afterward,
that I will pour out my Spirit on all flesh;
your sons and your daughters shall prophesy,
your old men shall dream dreams,
and your young men shall see
visions. —Joel 2:28 ESV

Dreams and visions are important parts of your inheritance as a child of God filled with the Holy Spirit. Whether they are dreams in the night or visions birthed in our hearts as we co-labor with God while we're awake, it's important to record and remember the important revelations we are receiving.

This journal is not an exhaustive resource, providing you different biblical strategies on dream interpretation. There are other materials and teachings available to provide you with instruction in those subjects. Rather, before you begin to receive interpretation and learn some of the practical ways to understand symbols, images, visions, pictures, and other such *dream language*, it is important for you to begin a personal practice of **writing down your dreams and visions.**

The purpose for this journal is to give you a place to record revelations and dreams from your quiet time with God. A large portion of this quiet time actually takes place as you are sleeping. This is why dreams are so important. At the same time, God also supernaturally communicates with us while we are awake through visions. When you get into the habit of writing down what God is speaking, you start to develop a consistent routine of recording your dreams and visions. Remember, God is *always* speaking. However, His native language is not English, Hebrew, or Greek. He speaks through many different ways. Two of the most common and biblical—that we tend to miss—are visions and dreams.

In the Old Testament, one of the signs that someone was *filled with the Spirit* was their ability to dream, and in turn, interpret that dream. Consider the examples of Daniel and Joseph. Both men dreamed dreams, and both men were acknowledged as ones who were filled with the Spirit of God (see Dan. 5:14; Gen. 41:38-39).

Consider this—you spend a significant portion of your life *sleeping*. Yet, even as you sleep, your heart and spirit are awake. They are still receiving.

The following is an excerpt from Bill Johnson's book, *Dreaming With God*, which reminds you of the importance of giving God your nights and preparing for the exciting dream journey that awaits you:

> *I try to end each day with my heart's affection stirred up and directed to the Holy Spirit. What an amazing way to go to sleep.*
>
> *The Song of Solomon reveals this poetically, "I sleep, but my heart is awake" (Song of Sol. 5:2). God loves to visit us in the night and give us instruction that we would have a hard time receiving during the day (see Job 33:15-16).*

Dream Journal

The desire to give God our night season flows naturally from the child's heart that knows revelation cannot be earned. Ask Him specifically to minister to you in the night through visions and dreams. Once you have a dream or vision, write it out, and ask Him for understanding.

You can begin your dream journey by praying the following:

Holy Spirit, I give you my days and my nights. I ask You to come and speak to me through my dreams and during my time alone with You.

Lord, Your Word says that dreams and visions are the inheritance for those who have received the Holy Spirit. Thank You, Father, that I have Your very Spirit dwelling within me, and that whether sleeping or awake, You are always speaking to me.

Help me to recognize Your voice.

Quicken my memory and help me to accurately record the images, pictures, and occurrences that I see through both visions and dreams.

Wake me in the night after a significant dream so I am able to write it down and record it while it is still fresh in my mind.

Lead me into Truth, granting me interpretation and understanding of what You are saying.

Help me to measure every dream and vision that I believe is from You by the standard of Your Word.

Dream Journal

Above all, help me to keep Jesus the center of any dream or vision I receive. May He receive great glory as I walk in this fresh experience of hearing Your voice.

Thank You, Jesus, for making it possible for me to hear God's voice. I know that in the Old Testament only a select few were able to be filled with Your Spirit and receive dreams and visions from Heaven. But now, because of Your blood, my sin has been blotted out and I have received Your precious Holy Spirit. The same Spirit who was upon Daniel and Joseph is now living inside of me! He will never leave me or forsake me, and He always speaking to me.

Grant me eyes to see, ears to hear, and a heart to understand what You are saying through my dreams and visions.

In Jesus' name, Amen.

You can actually pray this prayer before you go to sleep each night or as you get ready to spend time alone with God. Whether awake or asleep, He wants to communicate with you. He wants to reveal things to your heart. He wants to open your eyes in a greater way to see the *unseen*.

Posture your heart in a place of expectation to hear from Heaven and prepare yourself to receive and record all that God wants to speak to you.

Dream Journal

Jesus wants to shine through our lives; He wants out of the box.
Christ in us has the answers that those around us are waiting for.
—KEVIN DEDMON

Dream Journal

....
....
....
....
....
....
....
....
....
....
....
....
....
....
....
....
....
....
....
....

When we learn to receive from our spirit, our mind becomes
the student and is therefore subject to the Holy Spirit. That is
biblical learning—the spirit giving influence to the mind.

—BILL JOHNSON

Dream Journal

Because the renewal brought refreshing and the Father's heart was being poured out, I found myself, like so many others, lost in His amazing presence. I would go into a deep place of intimacy with Him.

—BENI JOHNSON

Dream Journal

Intimacy is the main purpose of prayer. And it's through relationship that God entrusts to us the secrets of His heart, that we might express them in prayer.

—BILL JOHNSON

Dream Journal

Likewise, the Spirit also helps in our weaknesses. For we do not know what we should pray for as we ought, but the Spirit Himself makes intercession for us with groanings which cannot be uttered.

—ROMANS 8:26

Dream Journal

It was also a time when the Holy Spirit stirred up my heart, releasing me to be who I am. ...In this time of stirring, I felt Him speak to me a word that would change my life, "I want you to carry joy and intercession."

—BENI JOHNSON

Dream Journal

When we pray for His Kingdom to come, we are asking Him to superimpose the rules, order, and benefits of His world over this one until this one looks like His.

—BILL JOHNSON

Dream Journal

We found that, once we experienced that depth of His love, we desired nothing on earth more than to be in the presence of our heavenly Father.

—BENI JOHNSON

Dream Journal

Each one of us is a treasure to God. He bought each one of us with a price: the precious blood of Jesus. And when we are finally found, there is rejoicing because collectively and individually we are His Ultimate Treasure!

—KEVIN DEDMON

Dream Journal

....

....

....

....

....

....

....

....

....

....

....

....

....

....

....

....

....

Jesus has called every believer to live a naturally supernatural life. We are called to do what Jesus did, to demonstrate the Good News through a natural lifestyle of signs and wonders.

—KEVIN DEDMON

Dream Journal

Faith is the mirror of the heart that reflects the realities of an unseen world—the actual substance of His Kingdom. Through the prayer of faith, we are able to pull the reality of His world into this one.

—BILL JOHNSON

Dream Journal

Deep calls unto deep at the noise of Your waterfalls; all Your waves and billows have gone over me.

—PSALM 42:7

Dream Journal

Prayer is the simplest activity of the believer. Child to Father...
lover to lover...conversation...sometimes spoken. Prayer is also
one of the more complicated issues for us. Formulas don't work
in this Kingdom relationship.

—BILL JOHNSON

Dream Journal

...God is preparing people everywhere through visions, dreams, and supernatural encounters.

—Kevin Dedmon

Dream Journal

...You must pay attention to the dreams and desires in your heart, because they will help you get in touch with the invitation God is extending to you to partner with Heaven and bring healing to the land.

—BANNING LIEBSCHER

Dream Journal

For I know the thoughts that I think toward you, says the Lord,
thoughts of peace and not of evil, to give you a future and a hope.
—JEREMIAH 29:11

Dream Journal

The blood of Jesus was not shed merely to save us from our sins, but to restore us to a relationship with God in which we partner with Him as kings and priests to bring the planet under His rule and reign.

—BILL JOHNSON

Dream Journal

God wants us to learn how to strengthen ourselves through Him because developing our skills will promote spiritual longevity.

—BILL JOHNSON

Dream Journal

Dreams were meant to come true.

—BANNING LIEBSCHER

Dream Journal

For the word of God is living and active, sharper than any two-edged sword, piercing to the division of soul and of spirit, of joints and of marrow, and discerning the thoughts and intentions of the heart.

—HEBREW 4:12

Dream Journal

Once in the middle of the night, God came in answer to my prayer for more of Him, yet not in a way I had expected. I went from a dead sleep to being wide-awake in a moment. Unexplainable power began to pulsate through my body, seemingly just shy of electrocution.

—BILL JOHNSON

Dream Journal

Surely the Lord God does nothing, unless He reveals His secret to His servants the prophets.

—AMOS 3:7

Dream Journal

The reason God is so excited to come when we call is that He
has adopted us as His sons and daughters. The revelation of who
God is to us as our Father will infuse our prayers with faith like
nothing else.

—BANNING LIEBSCHER

Dream Journal

Honor has fallen on hard times in our culture. We focus on our private relationships with God and have a hard time recognizing spiritual authority and considering others as more important than ourselves.

—DANNY SILK

Dream Journal

Jesus paid the price of our access to the Father, thereby granting us the freedom that comes from the truth we gain through that unlimited knowledge of His heart.

—BILL JOHNSON

Dream Journal

There is no question that spending time with God changes our desires. We always become like the one we worship.
—BILL JOHNSON

Dream Journal

...walk in the ways of your heart and...your eyes; but know that for all these God will bring you into judgment. ...remove sorrow from your heart and put away evil from your flesh....

—ECCLESIASTES 11:9-10

Dream Journal

...When God wants to initiate a new movement in history, God does not intervene directly, but sends us dreams and visions that can, if attended to, initiate a process.

—BANNING LIEBSCHER

Dream Journal

A reformation has begun. And at the heart of this great move of the Spirit is the total transformation of the people of God as they discover their true identity and purpose.

—BILL JOHNSON

Dream Journal

The supernatural is being restored once again to the Church. Signs, wonders, healings, and prophecy are becoming consistently demonstrated—not just in crusades, but in everyday life both inside and outside the church walls.

—BANNING LIEBSCHER

Dream Journal

Living a naturally supernatural life, releasing God's Kingdom, moving Heaven to earth, is a result of living a dynamic, intimate relationship with God.

—KEVIN DEDMON

Dream Journal

_____

_____

_____

_____

_____

_____

_____

_____

_____

_____

_____

_____

_____

_____

_____

_____

_____

_____

Thankfully, people throughout the Church are beginning to recognize and embrace the truth that every believer is eligible and, in fact, is called to walk in the anointing of the Holy Spirit.
—BANNING LIEBSCHER

Dream Journal

For God may speak in one way, or in another, yet man does not perceive it. In a dream, in a vision of the night, when deep sleep falls upon men, while slumbering on their beds, then He opens the ears of men, and seals their instruction

—JOB 33:14-16

Dream Journal

For too long our mindset has been one of inferiority and insignificance, and this attitude has neutralized our anointing to impact nations. We have allowed ourselves to be overwhelmed with the evil state of the world and have believed the lie that we can not make a difference.

—BANNING LIEBSCHER

Dream Journal

....

....

....

....

....

....

....

....

....

....

....

....

....

....

....

....

....

....

What leads people to repentance is the kindness of God, demonstrated through His people healing the sick, prophesying the secrets of people's hearts, revealing their true destiny, and setting people free to live a blessed life.

—KEVIN DEDMON

Dream Journal

The Ultimate Treasure is the people who are just waiting to be discovered. They are those who desperately, and often secretly, need a real encounter with God in order to meet the overwhelming needs of their lives and the unfulfilled desires of their hearts.

—KEVIN DEDMON

Dream Journal

....

....

....

....

....

....

....

....

....

....

....

....

....

....

....

....

....

....

We have the privilege of rediscovering God's original purpose for His people. We who long for this must pursue Him with reckless abandon.

—BILL JOHNSON

Dream Journal

While God has provided angels to assist us in our commission, I don't take the posture that we are to command angels. Some feel they have that liberty. However, I believe it is a dangerous proposition. There is reason to believe that they are to be commissioned by God Himself in response to our prayers.

—BILL JOHNSON

Dream Journal

Let the word of Christ dwell in you richly in all wisdom, teaching and admonishing one another in psalms and hymns and spiritual songs, singing with grace in your hearts to the Lord.

—COLOSSIANS 3:16

Dream Journal

The Holy Spirit has been given to us to communicate the plans and desires of the Father. The Holy Spirit does this through visions, dreams, prophetic words, words of wisdom, and words of knowledge.

—KEVIN DEDMON

Dream Journal

You see, God is a dreamer and He is looking for people who will dream His dreams with Him.

—BILL JOHNSON

Dream Journal

For by grace you have been saved through faith, and that not of yourselves; it is the gift of God.

—EPHESIANS 2:8

Dream Journal

...If there is joy in Heaven, it only makes sense that there should be joy on the earth as well. Joy should be the normal lifestyle for the Christian.

—KEVIN DEDMON

Dream Journal

A bottle is not completely full until it overflows. So it is with the Holy Spirit. Fullness is measured in overflow.

—BILL JOHNSON

Dream Journal

These things I have spoken to you, that in Me you may have peace. In the world you will have tribulation; but be of good cheer, I have overcome the world.

—JOHN 16:33

Dream Journal

I am convinced that God likes my ideas. So, when I pray, I pray from a place of security. I go into prayer believing that God is on my side.

—Beni Johnson

Dream Journal

Since thanksgiving keeps us sane and alive by connecting us to the Source of our life and purpose, it makes sense that Paul instructs us to give thanks "in everything."

—BILL JOHNSON

Dream Journal

Our dreams are not independent from God, but instead exist *because of* God. He lays out the agenda—*On earth as it is in Heaven*—and then releases us to run with it and make it happen!
—BILL JOHNSON

Dream Journal

Praying the Scriptures is a great way to pray the heart of God. I would read the verses over and over slowly. As I did, they began to go into my spirit. The Scriptures became alive in my spirit and mind. My prayers would come alive.

—BENI JOHNSON

Dream Journal

Prayers based on length and repetition are not the key to releasing God's Kingdom. ...Religious prayers are not the answer to changing the world.

—KEVIN DEDMON

Dream Journal

....
....
....
....
....
....
....
....
....
....
....
....
....
....
....
....

While there is no question that exposure to the miraculous
can help us grow in faith, such a demand is not a hunger for
Him but is instead an effort to put God on trial.

—BILL JOHNSON

Dream Journal

Effective prayer that brings Heaven to earth is about intimacy not performance, resting not striving, faith not formula, relationship not religion.

—Kevin Dedmon

Dream Journal

....
....
....
....
....
....
....
....
....
....
....
....
....
....
....
....

God is always talking to us, and we must incline our ear to hear
His voice. One of the most significant ways God speaks to me is
through dreams.

—BANNING LIEBSCHER

Dream Journal

....

....

....

....

....

....

....

....

....

....

....

....

....

....

How much more of God is there to know? In reality, no matter how much we already know and have experienced of God, there is always more because He is infinite.

—KEVIN DEDMON

Dream Journal

Your heart is the seat of your mind, imagination, will, desires, emotions, affections, memory, and conscience. It is also the center of your communion with the Spirit of God and possesses the faculties that perceive spiritual reality.

—BILL JOHNSON

Dream Journal

Therefore I say to you, whatever things you ask when you pray,
believe that you receive them, and you will have them.

—MARK 11:24

Dream Journal

A yielded imagination becomes a sanctified imagination; and it's the sanctified imagination that is positioned for visions and dreams.

—BILL JOHNSON

Dream Journal

Your destiny begins in your heart. The more you gaze on the face of Jesus with the eyes of your heart, the more you see who you are becoming.

—BILL JOHNSON

Dream Journal

Therefore do not cast away your confidence, which has great reward.

—HEBREWS 10:35

Dream Journal

Prayer will shift the atmosphere. And consistent prayer accesses realms of authority that nothing else can shake. All the resources and dominion of Heaven are available to us as we pray.

—Banning Liebscher

Dream Journal

Rejoice always, pray without ceasing, in everything give thanks; for this is the will of God in Christ Jesus for you.

—1 THESSALONIANS 5:16-18

Dream Journal

....

....

....

....

....

....

....

....

....

....

....

....

....

....

To work without fulfilled dreams and desires is to partner with the religious spirit that exalts routine without purpose, and calls it suffering. The honor of giving to promote ministry must not be devalued, but its emphasis should never be at the expense of each individual carrying their own creative expression of the Gospel through realizing their God-given dreams and desires.

—BILL JOHNSON

Dream Journal

An apostolic environment is an exciting place, because the focus on Heaven allows prayer, worship, miracles, signs, and wonders to become normal in our daily lives. However, there is one particular area that the role of apostle is not designed to address directly: the needs of people.

—DANNY SILK

Dream Journal

Scripture is clear that we have two options—we can choose either to protect the rules and create a religious culture, or to protect our relationships and create a culture of love.

—DANNY SILK

Dream Journal

But seek first the kingdom of God and His righteousness, and all these things will be added to you.

—Matthew 6:33

Dream Journal

Having our prayers answered is entirely a matter of knowing and trusting our Father. There is a level of confidence you will pray with when you know the goodness of the Father's heart; you have a boldness that knows His heart, that understands His will, and that He is faithful to answer.

—BANNING LIEBSCHER

Dream Journal

If any of you lacks wisdom, let him ask of God, who gives to all liberally and without reproach, and it will be given to him.

—JAMES 1:5

Dream Journal

Our hearts can embrace things that our heads can't. Our hearts will lead us where our logic would never dare to go. ...In the same way, true faith affects the mind. Faith does not come from our understanding. It comes from the heart.

—BILL JOHNSON

Dream Journal

_____
_____
_____
_____
_____
_____
_____
_____
_____
_____
_____
_____
_____
_____
_____
_____
_____
_____
_____
_____

The dynamic ways in which God speaks to the prophet including dreams, visions, and trances, create awareness of God's involvement with us. These supernatural tools introduce an infusion of sensitivity toward Heaven's activity and plans.

—DANNY SILK

Dream Journal

The prophet who has a dream, let him tell a dream; and he who has My word, let him speak My word faithfully....

—JEREMIAH 23:28

Dream Journal

The reason intimacy is so important is that the power to release signs and wonders, miracles, and healings comes out of the presence of God. ...we are like sponges, soaking up His presence, and when we walk through the world, we leak what we have received.

—Kevin Dedmon

Dream Journal

Learn the blessings that come with the power of God's ordered alignment: the inheritance of courage, wisdom, identity, protection, and an anointing for signs and wonders.

—BANNING LIEBSCHER

Dream Journal

Some, because of their fear of error, have said it's improper to seek an experience with God. ...At some point we must believe in a God who is big enough to keep us safe in our quest for more of Him.

—BILL JOHNSON

Dream Journal

When you lie down, you will not be afraid; yes, you will lie down and your sleep will be sweet.

—Proverbs 3:24

Dream Journal

What God has planned for the Church in this hour is greater than our ability to imagine and pray. We must have the help of the Holy Spirit to learn about these mysteries of the Church and God's Kingdom. Without Him we don't have enough insight even to know what to ask for in prayer.

—BILL JOHNSON

Dream Journal

...You will always find a tool—a prophetic word, a Scripture verse that has leapt out at you, a testimony, or a prayer strategy, for example—that God has put in your arsenal, something that provides a key to overcome the present situation.

—BILL JOHNSON

Dream Journal

I have rarely ever led someone to Christ through argument. Not because I cannot argue, but because at some point the debate requires a leap of faith, *"It is by grace you are saved, through faith"* (Eph. 2:8 NIV), not debate.

—KEVIN DEDMON

Dream Journal

The desire to give God our night season flows naturally from the child's heart that knows revelation cannot be earned. Ask Him specifically to minister to you in the night through visions and dreams.

—BILL JOHNSON

Dream Journal

As intercessors, we need to be focused in our prayers and our strategies. Effective intercessors know how to listen for the plays that God calls, and they know how to catch the ball and make the touchdown.

—BENI JOHNSON

Dream Journal

_____
_____
_____
_____
_____
_____
_____
_____
_____
_____
_____
_____
_____
_____
_____
_____

As part of the new breed, you must pay attention to the dreams in your heart because they are meaningful to God. Don't downplay the desires of your heart. God will use them to place you in society as an agent of restoration.

—BANNING LIEBSCHER

Dream Journal

Religion idolizes concepts and avoids personal experience.
Anything that will take the place of dependence upon the Holy
Spirit and His empowering work can be traced back to this spirit
of opposition.

—BILL JOHNSON

Dream Journal

Jesus continues to point the way to the Father. It has now become our job, by means of the Holy Spirit, to discover and display the Father's heart: giving life, and destroying the works of the devil.

—BILL JOHNSON

Dream Journal

....

....

....

....

....

....

....

....

....

....

....

....

....

....

....

....

....

....

Signs and wonders are needed to convince the world, but the object must always be to introduce them to a growing, personal, intimate, face-to-face, daily encounter with God.

—KEVIN DEDMON

Dream Journal

...God has set it up so that His dream of giving the nations to His Son as well as the dreams of His sons and daughters can only be fulfilled together. The passions of your heart are intimately and intrinsically linked to God's desire for nations being discipled and societies completely transformed!

—BANNING LIEBSCHER

Dream Journal

Jesus showed us how to spirit-fight. He broke down that worldly mindset by praying, preaching, and doing. ...When we think with a heavenly mindset, we begin to operate with an offensive lifestyle. God has given us the ball, which is the Word of God, now it is our responsibility to pass it on to others.

—BENI JOHNSON

Dream Journal

When we pray from the offensive lifestyle, our prayers are strong and mighty because we have spent so much time with God and He has stamped on our hearts who we are.

—BENI JOHNSON

Dream Journal

I want to encourage you that you can live a naturally supernatural life and do extraordinary feats as an ordinary Christian.
—Kevin Dedmon

Dream Journal

....

....

....

....

....

....

....

....

....

....

....

....

....

....

Any time we begin to feel weary in our prayers, the Lord is faithful and sends us a dream or a prophetic word or enlivens a Scripture for us, and faith to keep pressing in ignites again in our hearts. It is one of the most exciting, dynamic aspects of our interactions with the Lord. It makes prayer and adventure.

—BANNING LIEBSCHER

Dream Journal

And it shall come to pass in the last days, says God, That I will pour out of My Spirit on all flesh; your sons and your daughters shall prophesy, your young men shall see visions, your old men shall dream dreams.

—Acts 2:17

Dream Journal

We believe, as a people of God's power, that we are to bring Heaven to earth. Joy is a very big part of Heaven. Heaven is filled with joy. It is our responsibility to bring that here to earth.

—BENI JOHNSON

Dream Journal

Because rejoicing, prayer, and thanksgiving attract Heaven, they are vital tools for strengthening ourselves in the Lord.

—BILL JOHNSON

Dream Journal

....

....

....

....

....

....

....

....

....

....

....

....

....

....

....

....

God is extravagantly generous, and the life He has given us to experience on this planet is not a life of survival, but of abundance and blessing.

—BILL JOHNSON

Dream Journal

....

....

....

....

....

....

....

....

....

....

....

....

....

....

....

....

When any of us go into God's presence and tap into the realm
of Heaven, we position ourselves to receive great breakthroughs.
—BENI JOHNSON

Dream Journal

And whatever you ask in My name, that I will do, that the Father may be glorified in the Son. If you ask anything in My name, I will do it.

—John 14:13-14

Dream Journal

Sadly, some Christians view God as a benevolent absentee father who just sends the things we need and desire from afar. God desires to reveal Himself to His children ever day in face-to-face encounters.

—KEVIN DEDMON

Dream Journal

Once we have an up-close, personal relationship with God, the supernatural becomes a natural outflow.

—KEVIN DEDMON

Dream Journal

If we teach, preach, or witness and nothing happens, we must go back to the drawing board—our knees.

—BILL JOHNSON

Dream Journal

There is no account of Jesus ever taking a vacation. He is still working today. When you pray, you will never get a recorded message saying, "God is on vacation and will not be able to work a miracle until He gets back in two weeks. Until then, just hang in there and work it out yourself."

—KEVIN DEDMON

Dream Journal

When the eyes of the blind were opened and the person who had been deaf all of his life could hear for the first time, there was joy and excitement. This is where we need to live.

—Beni Johnson

Dream Journal

He's not the kind of Father who gives us a command to ask for something without fully intending to answer our request. He directs us to pray this prayer because it is in His heart to fulfill it. The safest prayers in existence are the ones He tells us to pray.

—BILL JOHNSON

Dream Journal

God's *yes* together with our *yes* is what brings about breakthrough in prayer. I'm continually amazed that God would choose to partner with us.

—BENI JOHNSON

Dream Journal

Jesus said to him, "I am the way, the truth, and the life. No one comes to the Father except through Me."

—JOHN 14:6

Dream Journal

When the Lord speaks to us through dreams, prophetic words, Scriptures, and other prophetic experiences, He's providing fuel for our fires of prayer. These things give direction and let us know we are on the right track.

—BANNING LIEBSCHER

Dream Journal

If we are going to be a people who pray with an offensive purpose, "hitting the mark" in our prayers, we must be on a quest to search the heart of God.

—BENI JOHNSON

Dream Journal

As God draws us into a place of embracing the realm of His mysteries, He establishes the life of faith in us. Hidden things are revealed to those who hunger for Him, and can recognize His voice.

—BILL JOHNSON

Dream Journal

It is a true statement that it's the hungry heart that hears best.
—Bill Johnson

Dream Journal

The dreams ingrained upon your heart are resident there because God wants to use you to bring revival in the particular realm of society you are zealous about.

—BANNING LIEBSCHER

Dream Journal

_____
_____
_____
_____
_____
_____
_____
_____
_____
_____
_____
_____
_____
_____
_____
_____
_____

The beauty of His will is lost for the person who does not know the language of the Spirit. It is vital to learn how God speaks.

—BILL JOHNSON

Dream Journal

....
....
....
....
....
....
....
....
....
....
....
....
....
....
....
....
....
....

The eyes of the Lord are on the righteous, and His ears are open to their cry.

—PSALM 34:15

Dream Journal

When I pray, He comes, and when He comes, He does good things because He is a good God in a good mood!
—KEVIN DEDMON

Dream Journal

It is not only possible for you and me to live a life of sustained passionate love, but it is achievable to live a life escalating in passion, to abide continually in the Lord's extreme love.

—BANNING LIEBSCHER

Dream Journal

The most natural thing in the Christian life is to be passionately in love with Jesus and for this blazing love to infuse all that we are and do.

—BANNING LIEBSCHER

Dream Journal

Remaining in Him has to do with resting in Him—resting in the work that He has provided for us, as well as resting in His presence.

—Kevin Dedmon

Dream Journal

Jesus is the One standing at the door knocking. We didn't find Jesus; He found us. He wasn't lost; we were lost. More importantly, God's quest in capturing your heart doesn't stop when you become saved. He is still in pursuit of you, even today!

—BANNING LIEBSCHER

Dream Journal

Praying always with all prayer and supplication in the Spirit, being watchful to this end with all perseverance and supplication for all the saints—

—EPHESIANS 6:18

Dream Journal

Most people already know what is wrong with them. What they do not know is what is *right* about them—what their destiny is in Christ, and the good plans and purposes He has for them.

—KEVIN DEDMON

Dream Journal

I will both lie down in peace, and sleep; for You alone, O Lord, make me dwell in safety.

—PSALM 4:8

Dream Journal

....
....
....
....
....
....
....
....
....
....
....
....
....
....
....

Words of knowledge let people know that God cares about their needs, no matter how seemingly insignificant or overwhelming their needs may be. They also communicate how God knows them in minute detail, which for many, proves that God exists and is interested in their lives.

—KEVIN DEDMON

Dream Journal

As God brings the generations together and these young people
connect with fathers and mothers, powerlessness will be replaced
with the strength and grace that begins to flower in their lives.
—BANNING LIEBSCHER

Dream Journal

If He [God] is to be free to move in our lives, we will constantly be involved in impossibilities. The supernatural is His natural realm.

—BILL JOHNSON

Dream Journal

I thought, "This is Heaven. This is what it feels like when you are in Heaven." Can you imagine what it will be like when we are in Heaven forever and all the clutter that fills our lives is gone? That's peace.

—BENI JOHNSON

Dream Journal

Biblical passion is a mysterious mixture of humility, supernatural hunger, and faith. I pursue because I have been pursued.

—BILL JOHNSON

Dream Journal

For many Christians, the idea of hearing from God is very foreign. Christians have no problem petitioning God, *expecting* Him to hear them. What they have difficulty with is believing that they hear from Him.

—KEVIN DEDMON

Dream Journal

The lack of miracles works like a thief, stealing precious revelation that is within the grasp of every man, woman, and child.

—BILL JOHNSON

Dream Journal

There is much suffering in this world. Jesus suffered. But Jesus knew where His strength was. He had experienced great joy in Heaven. All of Heaven is joy.

—BENI JOHNSON

Dream Journal

....

....

....

....

....

....

....

....

....

....

....

....

....

If we feed ourselves on life and joy and what God is doing here on earth, we will live like Jesus lived on earth. But, if we feed ourselves on bad news all of the time, if that is our focus in life, then we will live out of fear and despair.

—BENI JOHNSON

Dream Journal

Thanksgiving and praise are tools to strengthen ourselves not because they help us get something from the Lord, but because they reconnect us to our primary purpose—to minister to Him in worship.

—BILL JOHNSON

Dream Journal

When you learn how to strengthen yourself, you will reach your destiny, fulfill your God-born dreams, and become a person who can accurately represent Jesus....

—BILL JOHNSON

Dream Journal

....

....

....

....

....

....

....

....

....

....

....

....

....

....

....

....

....

....

....

....

....

Seize the moment; say yes to Jesus with all of your heart. He will use you in ways you never dreamed possible as you partner with Jesus to see Him receive the nations of the earth as His inheritance.
—BANNING LIEBSCHER

Dream Journal

_____

_____

_____

_____

_____

_____

_____

_____

_____

_____

_____

_____

_____

_____

_____

_____

_____

Over the years, I have found that the joy of the Lord, the medicine from Heaven, has been very effective in releasing the supernatural power of God.

—KEVIN DEDMON

Dream Journal

God desires to see His glory released. And all over the world, in every part of society, He is raising up prayer...in the midst of darkness.

—BANNING LIEBSCHER

Dream Journal

_____

There is an underlying mindset that Christians are not to live by
feelings, but by faith. True, feelings should not affect my faith,
but faith should affect my feelings.

—KEVIN DEDMON

Dream Journal

The prayer of faith that always gets results is the kind we can pray because we have drawn close to His heart and heard Him talk about what He wants to do.

—BILL JOHNSON

Dream Journal

Joy is the result of our redeemed heart reveling in its participation in God's unfolding plan for the earth through prayer.

—BILL JOHNSON

Dream Journal

Ask, and it will be given to you; seek, and you will find; knock, and it will be opened to you.

—Matthew 7:7

Dream Journal

When we do what He is doing, aligning our bodies as well as our spirits and souls with what He has said, there is a release of His nature that flows to us in that place of intimacy.

—BILL JOHNSON

Dream Journal

God's paramount goal for each of us is a heart awakened with love for Jesus that yields a life willing to sacrifice everything, and it can only happen through passion.

—BANNING LIEBSCHER

Dream Journal

You can't look at Him and then look back at your circumstances with the same perspective. Also, you can't experience the realm of His glory, which is His realm of supernatural provision, without receiving a measure of His grace and strength.

—BILL JOHNSON

Dream Journal

Sustaining prayer isn't so arduous when you believe God responds
to your prayer. You trust breakthrough will come because God
answers prayer. Our faith is not in our ability to pray but in His
ability to answer.

—BANNING LIEBSCHER

Dream Journal

His [God's] covenant brings peace, happiness, safety, and completeness, and it will never be taken from us. When He shows up, His presence is a safe place.

—Danny Silk

Dream Journal

_____

_____

_____

_____

_____

_____

_____

_____

_____

_____

_____

_____

_____

_____

_____

God awaits you and me in the secret place of prayer. There are distinctive realms available to us when we enter into His presence and intimately commune with Him.

—BANNING LIEBSCHER

Dream Journal

Heaven has what we want. Every creative dream is fulfilled in Heaven. The great news is that we have access to that realm through prayers of faith.

—BILL JOHNSON

Dream Journal

Sometimes we hope that peace means the absence of conflict, but true peace is always the result of victory.

—DANNY SILK

Dream Journal

Be joyful in hope, patient in affliction, faithful in prayer.
—ROMANS 12:12 NIV

Dream Journal

Someone gave me a helpful clue to discerning His voice; he said, "You know you've heard from God whenever you have an idea that's better than one you could think up yourself."

—BILL JOHNSON

Dream Journal

Visions come both to the natural eye and to the eyes of the heart. The second are the pictures in the mind, which are the visual equivalent of the still small voice—they are as easy to miss as they are to get.

—BILL JOHNSON

Dream Journal

There have been times when I have set out to do some praying with all of the best intentions, and God has whispered to me, "Not now" or "Don't touch that in prayer." It's not to put fear in us and to stop the ministry of our intercessions, but we need to be wise and learn to listen and be sensitive to the moving of the Holy Spirit.

—BENI JOHNSON

Dream Journal

Having the heart and the ability to hear from God leaves us with an
unlimited potential in resourcing earth with Heaven's resources.
—BILL JOHNSON

Dream Journal

When you say yes to Jesus while surrounded by other options, it establishes a deep conviction inside of you that cannot be easily shaken.

—BANNING LIEBSCHER

Dream Journal

...We find that while getting answers to prayer is wonderful and important, hearing His voice in the intimacy of prayer is the true source of our strength and life.

—BILL JOHNSON

Dream Journal

As important as having a daily time with the Lord is, it's not the ultimate goal. The objective is to have the affections of your heart pointed in His direction no matter what is going on.

—BANNING LIEBSCHER

Dream Journal

....

....

....

....

....

....

....

....

....

....

....

....

....

....

Over and over again He [God] woke me up in the middle of the
night to talk to me. Mostly I was expecting some incredibly deep
revelation that I would be able to teach, but each time He gently
said, "I just wanted to tell you I loved you."

—BANNING LIEBSCHER

Dream Journal

When we treasure His promises by holding them close to our heart and anchoring our soul in them through prayerful mediation, we are demonstrating that we believe they are true, and we are showing practical trust in the One who has given them to us.

—BILL JOHNSON

Dream Journal

Persistent prayer shapes our character, reinforces our tenacity, focuses our trust on the Lord, and increases our capacity to carry the authority and anointing that the Father has given us.

—BANNING LIEBSCHER

Dream Journal

Be anxious for nothing, but in everything by prayer and supplication, with thanksgiving, let your requests be made known to God; and the peace of God, which surpasses all understanding, will guard your hearts and minds through Christ Jesus.

—PHILIPPIANS 4:6-7

Dream Journal

We have opportunity to affect the direction and flow of history through our prayers and intercessions.

—BILL JOHNSON

Dream Journal

For with God nothing will be impossible.

—LUKE 1:37

Dream Journal

Miracles cause a shift in priorities. Without them, we are more inclined to be directed by our own minds and call it spirituality.
—BILL JOHNSON

Dream Journal

Prophets are forged in the deserts of fasting, not the deserts of feasting.

—Banning Liebscher

Dream Journal

....

....

....

....

....

....

....

....

....

....

....

....

....

....

....

....

Why is this important to understand [the house of God?] This revelation shows the resources that are at our disposal to carry out the Master's plan.

—BILL JOHNSON

Dream Journal

Prayer will shift the atmosphere. And consistent prayer accesses realms of authority that nothing else can shake.

—BANNING LIEBSCHER

Dream Journal

....

....

....

....

....

....

....

....

....

....

....

....

....

....

....

....

Why else would we give ourselves to prayer day and night? We can only do it if we know He longs to respond to our prayers.
—BANNING LIEBSCHER

Dream Journal

We are a people who have the incredible opportunity to change our environment. We have living within us the Holy Spirit. He is living in us so that we can be releasers of that power.

—BENI JOHNSON

Dream Journal

The fact that praying in the Spirit increases our ability to agree with God in prayer is the key to understanding how praying in the Spirit builds our faith.

—BILL JOHNSON

Dream Journal

One of the men in our church came to me with a dream he had. ...A group of women and I were taking care of problems with laughter and joy. We had a supernatural vacuum cleaner and... vacuumed the brokenness away. I just laughed and said, "Yes, that's how we pray."

—BENI JOHNSON

Dream Journal

And whatever things you ask in prayer, believing, you will receive.
—MATTHEW 21:22

Dream Journal

True heavenly experiences are always life changing. When I am having such an experience, it feels as though my whole being is awakened to that moment. Recently, I experienced a heavenly encounter where Jesus picked me up and swirled me around.

—BENI JOHNSON

Dream Journal

....
....
....
....
....
....
....
....
....
....
....
....
....
....

While this was all going on, there was a feeling that I had experienced before when I had been in God's presence. It was peace. ...the most complete peace that I had ever felt.

—BENI JOHNSON

Dream Journal

God sometimes speaks to us by hiding truths in phrases, stories, riddles, and circumstances. The meaning is there for us to find.

—BILL JOHNSON

...A young dreamer generation is rising, and their dreams are from Heaven. ...God, the greatest counter-cultural Dreamer, is commissioning them to release the roar: *I have a dream and let my people go.*

—Banning Liebscher

Dream Journal

Heaven is begging to invade the prison so many people live in, whether it is depression, pain, disease, or fear. Our role is to eliminate those things in our lives, homes, and church communities so we can lead others to the peace, joy, freedom, and love we've found for ourselves.

—DANNY SILK

And even though the world around us is in the midst of drowning, they have not come to us because we look exactly like them. It is time for us to have such an encounter with God that our identity changes.

—BANNING LIEBSCHER

Dream Journal

I believe angels have been bored because we live the kind of lifestyles that don't require much of their help. Their assignment is to assist us in supernatural endeavors. If we are not people of risk, then there is little room for the supernatural.

—BILL JOHNSON

Dream Journal

As I was praying, I could sense a shift in the atmosphere of our prayers and they seemed to transition from the strength of a small hammer to a power-loaded, demolition jackhammer!

—BANNING LIEBSCHER

Dream Journal

God encounters can be stunning experiences or the simple moments of being immersed in His peace; but they are markers along the journey of, "Thy kingdom come...."

—BILL JOHNSON

Dream Journal

_____

_____

_____

_____

_____

_____

_____

_____

_____

_____

_____

_____

_____

_____

As you tap into the love that is yours, you will begin to see people with God's loving eyes. Instead of praying or speaking words of death, you will begin to pray and speak words of life and love.
—BENI JOHNSON

Dream Journal

_____
_____
_____
_____
_____
_____
_____
_____
_____
_____
_____
_____
_____
_____
_____
_____
_____

We've been given the capacity to dream and, more importantly,
to dream with God. His language continues to be unveiled, His
heart is being imparted, and permission has been given to try to
exaggerate His goodness.

—BILL JOHNSON

Dream Journal

When I spend time in the secret place, alone with God, I become so wrapped up in His presence that every other desire loses its importance to me. In that place, I have found myself "caught up" in many different types of mystical experiences.

—BENI JOHNSON

Dream Journal

Awareness of unseen things is a vital aspect of the Christian life.
...What I know will help me What I think I know will hurt me.
It's the spirit of revelation that helps me know the difference.

—BILL JOHNSON

Dream Journal

....

....

....

....

....

....

....

....

....

....

....

....

....

....

....

....

....

....

....

....

....

....

Revelation is not poured out to make us smarter. Revelation leads to a God encounter, and that encounter forever changes us.
—BILL JOHNSON

Dream Journal

...I will pray with the spirit, and I will also pray with the understanding. I will sing with the spirit, and I will also sing with the understanding.

—1 Corinthians 14:15

Dream Journal

One of the assignments of the Holy Spirit is to let us know what is to come...and to discover what lies in the depths of God's heart for us.

—BILL JOHNSON

Dream Journal

_____
_____
_____
_____
_____
_____
_____
_____
_____
_____
_____
_____
_____
_____
_____
_____
_____
_____

Our job is not to spend all of our time worrying about the enemy's strategies. We are to make the plays that God calls. ...Don't allow the enemy to bring distraction. Make a choice not to partner with fear.

—BENI JOHNSON

Dream Journal

We must become the ongoing manifestation of revival and stop waiting for outside circumstances to line up with our dreams. We do this by giving thanks and rejoicing, praying as He prays, meditating on promises and testimonies, and associating with people of faith—not just when others around us are doing so, but continuously, as a lifestyle.

—BILL JOHNSON

Dream Journal

Tonight, as you lay your head on your pillow, let all of the stuff from your day just fall off, and begin to think on Him. Read a verse or pick a word that describes Him and begin to connect your spirit with His. You will begin to understand His world.

—BENI JOHNSON

Recommended Reading

Dreaming With God by Bill Johnson
When Heaven Invades Earth by Bill Johnson
Strengthen Yourself in the Lord by Bill Johnson
The Happy Intercessor by Beni Johnson
The Ultimate Treasure Hunt by Kevin Dedmon
Unlocking Heaven by Kevin Dedmon
Jesus Culture by Banning Liebscher
Culture of Honor by Danny Silk